Quiz: 63017

Level: 3.5

Points: .5

Veterans Day

Seven Oaks Elementary
Media Center

By Jacqueline S. Cotton

Consultants
Nanci Vargus, Ed.D.
Primary Multiage Teacher
Decatur Township Schools, Indianapolis, Indiana

Katharine A. Kane, Reading Specialist
Former Language Arts Coordinator
San Diego County Office of Education

Children's Press®
A Division of Scholastic Inc.
New York   Toronto   London   Auckland   Sydney
Mexico City   New Delhi   Hong Kong
Danbury, Connecticut

Designer: Herman Adler Design
Photo Researcher: Caroline Anderson
The photo on the cover shows a Veterans Day parade.

Library of Congress Cataloging-in-Publication Data

Cotton, Jacqueline S.
   Veterans Day / by Jacqueline S. Cotton.
      p. cm.
Includes index.
Summary: Explains the history of Veterans Day and why it is observed, and
suggests ways of honoring veterans on this special day, such as flying the flag,
attending parades, buying poppies, and visiting hospitals.
   ISBN 0-516-22672-X (lib. bdg.)   0-516-27499-6 (pbk.)
   1. Veterans Day—Juvenile literature. 2. Holidays—Juvenile literature.
[1. Veterans Day. 2. Holidays.] I. Title.
   D671 .C68 2002
   394.264–dc21   2002007387

©2002 Children's Press
A Division of Scholastic Inc.
All rights reserved. Published simultaneously in Canada.
Printed in China.

18 19 20 R 14 13 12   62

Do you know a veteran?

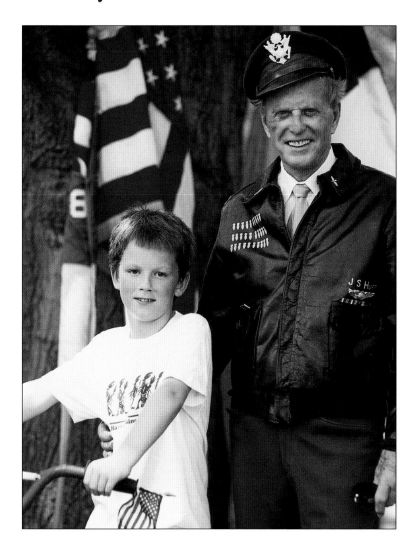

Veterans are men and women who were in the armed forces—the Army, Navy, Air Force, Marines, or Coast Guard.

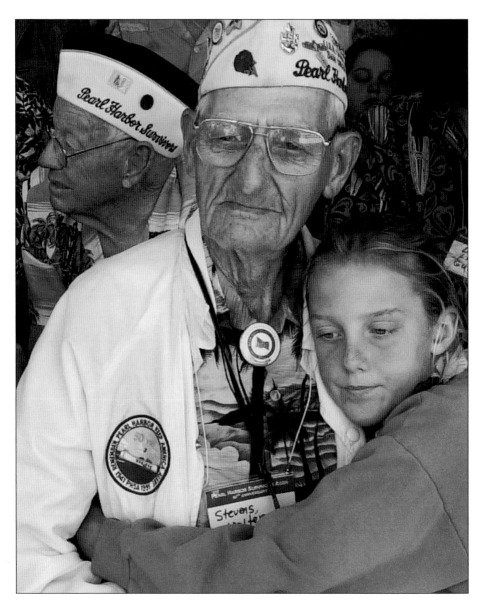

6

Veterans worked hard to keep our country a safe place to live.

On Veterans Day, Americans show that they are thankful for these men and women.

We celebrate Veterans Day
on November 11.

November 2012

Sunday	Monday	Tuesday	Wednesday	Thursday	Friday	Saturday
				1	2	3
4	5	6	7	8	9	10
11	12	13	14	15	16	17
18	19	20	21	22	23	24
25	26	27	28	29	30	

10

Veterans Day was first called Armistice Day. Armistice Day began after World War I ended on November 11, 1918.

Armistice Day was a day to remember the veterans from World War I. America fought in other wars after World War I, so Armistice Day was renamed Veterans Day.

13

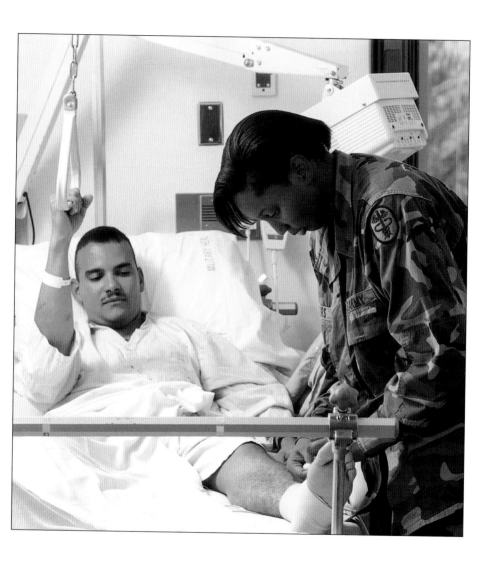

14

Veterans Day is not just
for people who fought in
wars. We also remember
the people who kept
our country safe in times
of peace.

People in the armed forces
also perform many other
jobs for which we should
be thankful.

People have different ways of showing veterans that they are thankful. Some people visit veterans in hospitals.

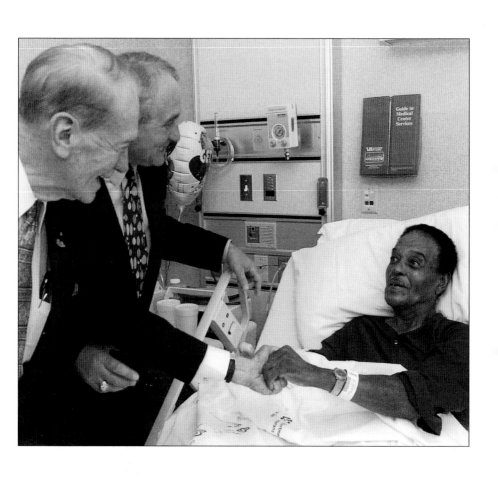

17

People go to Veterans
Day parades. They watch
veterans march.

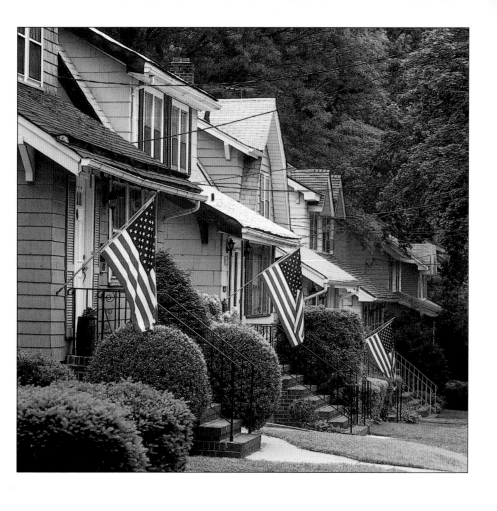

Some people fly flags
outside their homes.

Many people buy bright red paper poppies. Veterans sell these red flowers to help veterans and their families. These paper flowers look like the poppies on the World War I battlefields.

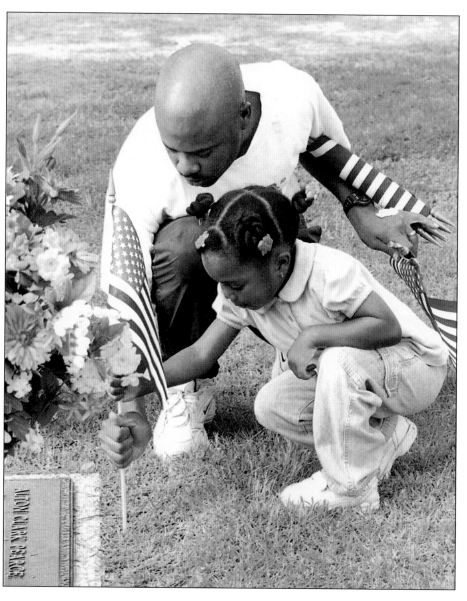

22

On Veterans Day, many people visit cemeteries. They put flowers and flags on veterans' graves.

At 11 o'clock in the morning on November 11, many people stay silent for two minutes. They remember those people who died to help protect our country.

25

The President of the United States places a wreath at the Tomb of the Unknowns in Arlington National Cemetery on Veterans Day.

This wreath honors all men and women who lost their lives in wars.

You do not have to know veterans to thank and remember them. These men and women protected our country and made it a safe place to live.

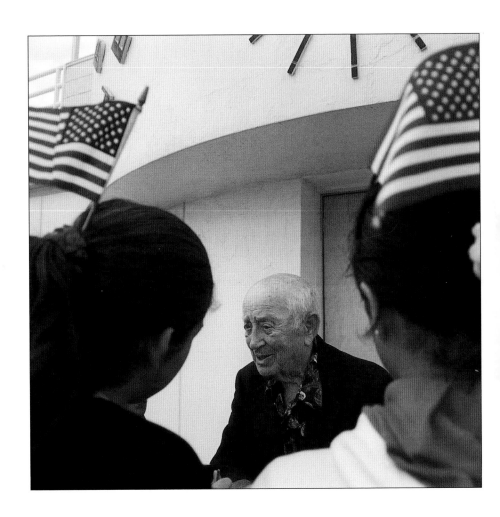

29

Words You Know

Armistice Day

cemetery

flags

hospital

30

parade

poppy

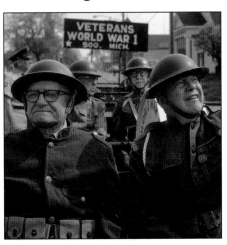

veterans

wreath

31

Index

About the Author

Jacqueline S. Cotton is a writer. She lives in Idaho with her husband Anthony and son Zachary.

Photo Credits

Photographs © 2002: AP/Wide World Photos: 26, 31 bottom right (Ron Edmonds), 25 (David Guttenfelder), 22, 30 top right (Kaye Nesbit/Argus), 17, 30 bottom right (Rogelio Solis), 10, 30 top left; Corbis Images/James L. Amos: 13, 31 bottom left; Folio, Inc.: 5 (Rob Crandall), 14 (Ira Wexler); Getty Images/Jeff Widener: 6; H. Armstrong Roberts, Inc./L. Powers: 3; Photo Researchers, NY: 19, 30 bottom left (George E. Jones), 21, 31 top right (Joseph Sohm/Chromosohm); Rigoberto Quinteros: cover; Visuals Unlimited: 29 (Jeff Greenberg), 18, 31 top left (D. Newman).